Skyhorse Publishing books may be purchased in bulk at special discounts for sales promotion, corporate gifts, fund-raising, or educational purposes. Special editions can also be created to specifications. For details, contact the Special Sales Department, Skyhorse Publishing, 307 West 36th Street, 11th Floor, New York, NY 10018 or info@skyhorsepublishing.com.

Skyhorse® and Skyhorse Publishing® are registered trademarks of Skyhorse Publishing, Inc.®, a Delaware corporation.

www.skyhorsepublishing.com

10 9 8 7 6 5 4 3 2 1

Library of Congress Cataloging-in-Publication Data is available on file.

ISBN: 978-1-62636-022-8

Printed in China.

We would like to thank:

Semic, our lovely Swedish publisher who gives us free reign and publishes our books.

—Thanks Semic, we love working with you!

Järbo Garn, who has yet again provided us with beautiful yarn.

—Thank you Järbo for a great collaboration!

Photographer Magnus Selander

—Magnus, you've done it again! Thank you for the fantastic photos.

Our readers

—Thanks to all of you who read our books. We hope we've inspired you.

As usual, we thank each other ☺

—Thanks, Susanna! What would I do without you?
—Same to you, Sania!

Fun with Yarn
and Fabric

Susanna Zacke & Sania Hedengren | Photos by Magnus Selander

Translated by Ellen Hedström

Skyhorse Publishing

We can't leave our balls of wool and piles of material alone . . .

. . . and this resulted in a new book! We've only included things that we personally like and find attractive. Most of it is improvised—we don't normally plan!—but we've found that the best results come when you don't spend too much time worrying about how it will turn out.

We've sewn many fun and useful things for the home: Among other things, pretty curtains made of lace tablecloths, colorful seat cushions, pillows, and bunting. A lot of what we make comes from old materials, such as a patchwork quilt made from '70s era retro sheets. We've done a lot of simple embroidery as well. You'll also discover crocheted vases, blankets, ottomans, and rugs.

Yes, the granny square is still here, but now it's accompanied by the lovely African flower, which we just love! We've also found the time for some tips on interior decorating, as well as decorations for Christmastime.

What we're saying is simply this: Have a flip through the book, read, take it all in, and be INSPIRED!

Good luck!

Sania & Susanna

Contents

A basket filled with pretty colored yarn adds a nice touch to your home.

Crocheted & a Bit of Knitted

We just keep on crocheting, so this is what we'll start with. The granny square is still our favorite, and it crops up in many of the projects in this book. A new acquaintance is the crocheted flower known as the "African flower"; we fell in love with it straight away. It's so much fun to crochet flowers and squares that it's really hard to stop—almost impossible. Try it and you'll see! So crochet for yourself, your home, your car . . .

Granny squares

We'll start off by explaining how to crochet a granny square, as so much in this book is based around this popular square. These directions will be the basis for any project that features one or more granny square. Using a thin yarn and a thin crochet hook to crochet the square works just as well as using thick yarn with a thick hook.

The granny square is a brilliant concept. In the olden days it was a way to utilize yarn remnants, and the color combinations are essentially limitless. According to your preference and need, you can also vary the size of the squares. You can make one huge square or a number of small ones depending on what you're planning on using them for.

Follow our instructions and learn how to make a granny square. You won't be disappointed!

We're still crazy about yarn!

How to Crochet a Granny Square

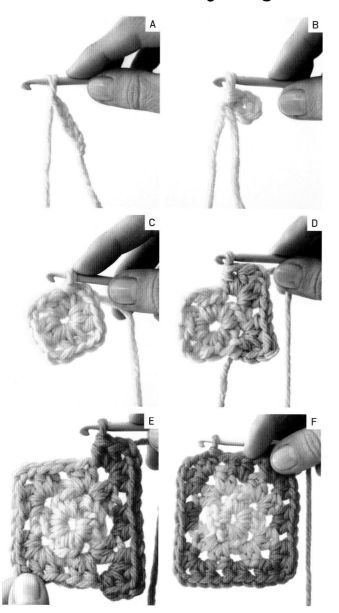

A. Work 5 chain stitches using a size 8/H hook. We used Molly as our yarn.

B. Make a closed ring by making a slip stitch in the first chain stitch.

C. Make 2 half double crochets into the circle, make 2 chain stitches and 2 half double crochets, 2 chain stitches, and repeat twice more. Attach the chain stitch with a slip stitch and cut the yarn. You should now be left with a square of chain stitches that makes a corner.

D. Switch to another color and make 2 half double crochets in one corner, make 2 chain stitches and 2 half double crochets in the same corner. To move to the next corner make 1 chain stitch. Make 2 half double crochets, 2 chain stitches, 2 half double crochets, and then 1 chain stitch to take you to the next corner. Continue in this fashion for the next 2 corners and end with a chain stitch. Attach with a slip stitch and cut the yarn.

E. Change color and crochet the next row in the same fashion. Make 2 half double crochets in one corner, make 2 chain stitches, and 2 half double crochets in the same corner. Make 1 chain stitch and then crochet 2 half double crochets in the next hole. Make 1 chain stitch. You are now in the next corner. Make 1 chain stitch and then 2 half double crochets, 2 chain stitches, and 2 half double crochets.

F. Continue for the whole round and finish off with a chain stitch. Attach with a slip stitch. If you want a larger square, continue making more rounds in the same manner.

Learn to knit a granny square. You won't regret it.

For aesthetic reasons, we always crotchet the last round of each of the squares in the same color.

Place the squares flat and sew together using overcast stitching.

11

Grandma's Quilt

A classic quilt made from granny squares is the most expected project in our book. We used this quilt as a key feature to decorate our glass veranda. The colors and style of the quilt inspired us to decorate using a mix of old and new and blending bold colors with white.

For this quilt, we used Raggi as our yarn and an 8/H crochet hook.

Crochet the granny squares according to the pattern on page 10.

Mix the colors according to your own taste. We ended each square with yarn of a natural white color.

Make the squares to your desired size. Ours measured 8½ x 8½ inches (22 x 22 cm).

Sew the squares together using overcast stitching.

Each square is made with a different color combination, so the look never gets repetitive. You'll find yourself wanting to crochet all the time so you can test out new combinations.

12

A pretty still life image with a flower, some old trinkets, and our colorful quilt.

A Little Bag

Bag

Cast on about 20 stitches using Hoooked Zpagetti and size 15 knitting needles. Knit in garter stitch until the piece measures roughly 20 inches (50 cm) or the desired length.

Fold the piece and sew the edges together.

Turn the bag the right way around.

Sew on a pot holder for decoration.

A little knitted bag with a crocheted edge makes a very cute piece to hang on a door handle. A pretty pot holder (we bought this one at a thrift store) can be used to adorn the center of the bag. The bag is knitted using a material called "Hoooked Zpagetti"; despite the fancy name, Hoooked Zpagetti is made from clothing remnants from clothing manufacturers. It feels especially good to make something from material that would otherwise be thrown away.

Handle

Using crochet hook P, crochet about 30 chain stitches, or the amount to get the desired length for the handle.

Turn using 1 chain stitch and then crochet the whole round using single crotchet. Make another handle following the same method.

Sew the handles onto the inside of the bag.

Edge

Crochet two rounds in single crochet using Molly yarn in your choice of color and hook 8/H. The last round is made as follows: Make 1 single crochet, skip a stitch, make 5 double crochets in the following single crochet, make 1 single crochet in the subsequent single crochet, skip a stitch, make 5 double crochets in the next single crochet and repeat until the end of the round. End the round with a slip stitch. Cut the yarn, pull through, and secure.

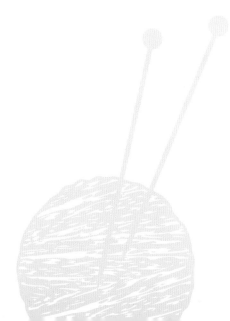

This little bag is more for decoration than it is for daily use, but you can use it if you don't need to carry too much.

The pot holder is a thrift store discovery and is a good example of repurposing something old.

This glass vase
looks much more
charming with its
new crocheted
cover.

16

A Crocheted Vase

A basic cylinder-shaped glass vase looks great with a crocheted cover made from Hoooked Zpagetti. As an embellishment, we sewed on a border of small granny squares. We also crocheted a base but it works just as well without one.

Make about 30 chain stitches using crochet hook P. Make a closed ring with a slip stitch in the first chain stitch. Measure the vase so that the cover is the right size. Now make 30 single crochets to get roughly 8 inches (20 cm) or the desired length.

The base

Crochet 5 chain stitches using crochet hook P and make a closed ring with a slip stitch in the first chain stitch.

Row 1: Make 8 single crochets by going into the ring.

Row 2: Make 2 single crochets in every single crochet. You should now have 16 single crochets.

Row 3–6: Increase by 8 single crochets evenly spread on each row.

Adjust the base so that it fits your vase. Ours is about 7 inches (18 cm) in diameter.

Sew the base onto the cover and turn it the right way around.

Granny squares

Crochet the granny squares according to the description on page 10. We used Soft Cotton yarn and hook 4/E. Every square consists of three rounds and the last round is made with a beige yarn. Sew together the squares (we made 10 of them) to make a border. Sew the border onto the vase cover.

Strong, clear colors work best when paired with a lot of white.

Large Granny Squares

This bedspread is one enormous granny square. It's a great example of how we improvise when we work. One of us simply started to crochet a granny square around Easter time and kept plugging along every evening until midsummer—when it measured around 8 x 8 ft (2.5 x 2.5 m) and consisted of 70 rounds! Well, it was perfect for a bedspread.

Start the granny square according to the description on page 10.

We used Molly yarn and an 8/H hook.

Continue to crochet as many rounds as you're up for. This massive square consists of 70 rounds.

This gigantic granny square makes a cozy bedspread. It was so much fun to make, so why not give it a try!

Molly yarn comes in many lovely colors, and mixing them all together results in a display that will boost your spirits whenever you look at it.

A Lovely Edge

We made a standard pink quilt unique by adding a crocheted edge. As the edge was already stitched, it was easy to crochet onto it.

Crochet a round of single crochets around the whole quilt.

Change color, and crochet the last round as follows: Crochet one single crochet and skip a stitch, make 5 double crochets in the following single crochet, skip a stitch, make 1 single crochet in the subsequent single crochet, skip a stitch, make 5 double crochets in the next single crochet, and repeat until the end of the round.

End the round with a slip stitch.

Cut the yarn, pull through, and secure.

We "pimped out" the quilt by adding a crocheted edge.

Crocheting Tealight Covers

Here's a quick project that's easy to do: Making little covers for glass tealight holders. Choose your favorite colors. Feel free to make several holders, so you can group your tealights together.

Gather your friends and crochet together.

We used Soft Cotton yarn and a 4/E hook.

Make about 10 chain stitches—measured according to the candle holders you are using. Make a closed ring with a slip stitch in the first chain stitch. Make 10 single crochets for 8 rounds or as many as needed to get the desired length and height.

Change color according to your preference. Cut the yarn and pull through.

Secure the yarn.

Slip onto the tealight holder.

These are the cutest candle holders and you can make them yourself quickly and easily.

Knitted white
vases holding
roses make an
attractive still life
image.

A Knitted Vase

Have a go at knitting a couple of covers for
your vases. It's a good starter project for
those new to knitting.

It's a very easy and a very quick project.
Give a vase like this as a present with a
bunch of flowers and your thoughtfulness
will definitely be appreciated.

~~~~~~~~~~~~~~~~~~~~~~~~~~~~~~

Cast on the desired number of stitches with
Lovikka yarn using size 13 needles. Measure the
vase and adjust the number of stitches as needed
for the size of the vase. Knit in garter stitch until
the piece is the same height as the vase. Bind off
and sew together.

We used Vinga yarn and hook 8/H.

Crochet granny squares according to the instructions on page 10.

These squares were made by crocheting 13 rounds, but you should measure the headrests in your car.

Mix the colors according to your own taste; we made the back piece in a solid color.

Place the finished back piece and front piece together with the right sides toward each other.

Sew the squares together using overcast stitching along three sides.

Turn the right way around and place on the headrest.

Crochet something unusual! We made covers for the headrests in the car.

The inside of the car looks positively delightful with crocheted covers for the headrests.

Hats for the Car

Why not? Another example of what you can do with a couple of granny squares. The car's dark and dull interior was jazzed up with colorful hats that we placed over the headrests—a detail that invites many a smile. The granny squares were sewn together in twos and then we were ready to roll.

Embellishing with Yarn

You can make your old clothes feel like new again by crocheting a few accessories for them. Here, a denim skirt was embellished with a few small granny squares and a '70s style crocheted belt.

For the squares and belt we used Soft Cotton yarn and a 4/E hook.

Crochet the granny squares according to the instructions on page 10.

Mix the colors according to your taste.

Sew the squares onto the skirt.

Belt:

Crochet about 170 chain stitches, or as many as you need to get the desired length.

Crochet four rounds in the same way:
1 chain stitch and then single crochets. The more rounds you do, the wider the belt. Change color according to your own taste.

Floor Cushion

The round tablecloth with this fantastic pattern is a secondhand bargain.

A floor cushion is perfect for when you need extra seating. This cushion was made from remnants and was totally improvised. We started crocheting with a thin yarn in the middle, and then used thicker yarn, and finished off with strips of cloth. For the base we used a round tablecloth that we bought at a thrift store.

We started off with Lady yarn and a 4/E hook.

Crochet 5 chain stitches and make a closed ring with a slip stitch in the first chain stitch.

Round 1: Make 8 single crochets by going into the ring.

Round 2: Make 2 single crochets in every single crochet.

Rounds 3–25: Increase by 8 single crochets, spread evenly on every round.

Change color according to your own taste.

Continue along the same way with Molly yarn in white and hook 8/H for 10 rounds.

Change to Hoooked Zpagetti and crochet hook P and crochet in the same way for 8 rounds.

The last 5 rounds are made in the same way with hook 17 and strips of fabric.

(You can find out more about fabric strips on page 35).

The top part is now finished.

Measure and cut a piece of fabric for the bottom part. Both parts should be of equal size but add about a 1 inch (3 cm) seam allowance.

Sew together the top and bottom parts, right sides together, leaving a 12 inch (30 cm) gap.

Turn the cushion the right way around.

Fill the cushion with something soft—filling from IKEA's cheap pillows is a cost-effective alternative.

Sew together the opening to close the cushion.

A cozy floor cushion created with remnants.

For the base we used an old tablecloth and sewed the parts together with a sewing machine.

Make something new from something old.

African Flower

For the poncho we used Soft Cotton yarn and a 4/E hook.

We made 60 flowers that were all finished off in beige. They were then sewn together to make a poncho.

Crochet the flowers according to the instructions on page 28.

We think the crocheted flower known as the African flower is wonderful.

Our new hobby is to crochet flowers known as "African flowers." Just like with granny squares, the color combinations are incredibly varied. African flowers are also very versatile. They can be used for cushion covers, quilts, shawls, scarves, furniture covers, decorations, ponchos, hats . . .

We promise you, you won't be able to stop crocheting flowers once you've gotten started!

The shape of
the flower was
perfectly suited
for making a
poncho, and
doesn't it look
amazing?

How to Crochet an African Flower:

A. Crochet 5 chain stitches.

B. Make a closed ring with a slip stitch in the first chain stitch.

C. Crochet in the ring of chain stitches: 2 double crochets, 1 chain stitch, 6 times.

D. Change color. Crochet into every chain stitch: 2 double crochets, 1 chain stitch, 2 double crochets, 6 times.

E. Crochet into every chain stitch: 7 double crochets.

F. Change color. Crochet 1 single crochet into every double crochet and between every flower petal make 1 double crochet—do this by going into the ring between the two groups of 2 double crochets.

G. Change color. 1 double crochet in every single crochet except in the center of every petal, where you make a double crochet, 1 chain stitch, 1 double crochet in the same single crochet making the corners of the hexagon.

Cut and secure the threads to finish off your flower.

Revitalize a cardigan with a crocheted trim.

With its new trim, this cardigan is entirely unique!

These cute wooden buttons were found in a toy shop.

A Cardigan with Trim

A quick way to put your own stamp on a knitted item of clothing that you've bought is to crochet a trim onto it. This cardigan was bought cheap at a large clothing chain, and of course, there are thousands in the same style. However, adding the trim along the bottom and around the sleeves makes it unique. Swapping the buttons is also easy to do . . .

For the crocheted trim we used Lady yarn and a 4/E hook.

Crochet 8 rounds of single crochets along the edge of the cardigan.

Change color according to your own taste.

The last round is crocheted in the following way:
Make 1 single crochet, 6 double crochets in the next single crochet, 1 single crochet, 6 double crochets in the subsequent single crochet and repeat to the end of the round.

Finish the round with a slip stitch.

Cut the yarn, pull through, and secure.

Creative Cushion

If you either don't want to, or don't have the time or energy to crochet many flowers, you can just as easily make a few flowers, sew them together, and then sew them onto a cushion as an embellishment. Even a single flower is just as decorative!

We used Soft Cotton yarn and a 4/E hook.

Crochet seven flowers according to the description on page 28. Sew them together into one piece, and then sew this piece onto a cushion cover.

A turquoise velvet cushion embellished with African flowers.

Decorate your home with a basketful of yarn.

Flowery Footstool

Here's another idea for your crocheted flowers. The footstool from IKEA will no longer look like a footstool from IKEA.

The footstool becomes a work of art, giving any room a classy look.

For the stool we used Soft Cotton yarn and a 4/E hook.

We made about 40 flowers that we finished off with white yarn. We then sewed them together to make the footstool cover. You have to try to tailor the cover to the footstool, and sometimes you'll need to move the flowers around a bit. It's a matter of testing your way forward with this one.

Make the flowers according to the description on page 28.

33

For some extra detailing, you can make the edge of the rug wavy.

Crochet a wavy edge like this:

Crochet 1 single crochet, skip a stitch, make 6 double crochets in the following single crochet, 1 single crochet in the subsequent single crochet, skip a stitch, make 6 double crochets in the next single crochet, and repeat until the end of the round. Finish the round with a slip stitch.

Cozy rugs that you can place anywhere you fancy. These look good in the bathroom or by your bed, or why not in the outhouse at your summer cottage.

Crocheted Rag Rugs

Crocheting round rag rugs like these is a quick and rewarding job. The crocheting can be heavy going at times but it's well worth it. We crocheted with scraps of old sheets and mixed them with Hoooked Zpagetti. Let your imagination guide you to design your own rugs!

~~~~~~~~~~~~~~~~~~~~

This is how you make the scraps of material:

Rip ½ inch (1 cm) wide strips of fabric following the direction of the grain. Don't rip all the way—keep about ½ inch (1 cm) at the end and then rip a strip going the other direction. In this way you avoid joining the strips.

Make 5 chain stitches using hook 17 and make a closed ring with 1 slip stitch in the first chain stitch.

Round 1: Make 8 single crochets by going into the ring.

Round 2: Make 2 single crochets in every single crochet. You should now have 16 single crochets.

Rounds 3–25: Increase by 8 single crochets, evenly divided on every round.

Change fabric/color/yarn according to your taste.

Adjust the increase with more or fewer stitches if you think it's needed. This depends on how thick the fabric is.

Finish off with a slip stitch, cut, and secure the yarn/strip.

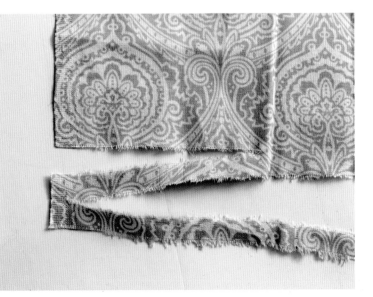

Embroidered & Embellished

Making handicrafts is a lot of fun and it's now more popular than ever. Maybe people used to see handicrafts as something that only old ladies do, but this is no longer how it's viewed. You can now see people embroidering cross stitch all over the place. We really want to inspire people to do more embroidery and decorating, and we want to show you our way—the simple way. You can embroider shoes, sew lettering onto pillows, decorate clothes with ribbon, and lots more. So get going—everyone can do it!

Delightful cotton spools inspire you to embroider.

Super cute hangers
that were fun to make.

Decorate clothes,
furniture, and
items with pretty
ribbons.

Heavenly Hangers

Wrapping material around things can make them look really cute
and decorative. Look around your home: Is there anything there
that can be wrapped? We've chosen to stick to smaller projects,
such as the guest hangers in the hall. They'll always hang there
for people to admire. You might find both the hangers and the
fabric for cheap at a thrift store.

Rip the fabric into roughly
1 inch (2 cm) thick pieces.

Dab a thin layer of glue on
the hanger.

Wind the fabric around
the entire hanger to
cover it.

Embroidered Slippers

Search your cupboards and chests of drawers for things to embroider. You'll probably find quite a few things—both clothes and other items that can be jazzed up with a little embroidery. Cross stitch is rewarding to do, and you can find inspiration and patterns online. Or you can make up your own patterns. To get the cross stitch even, it's good if the fabric is rough so that you can use the squares that naturally occur in the material. If not, cut a piece of needlepoint canvas, pin it on, and sew onto this.

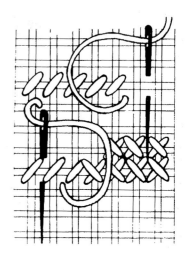

These slippers are getting a kurbit inspired pattern using cross stitch.

Follow these instructions to sew in cross stitch: In the square, push the needle up through the bottom left corner and then down in the top right hand corner and up through the fabric in the next square's left corner. You now have half a cross stitch. Repeat until you have a row of half cross stitches. Turn so that the thread is at the bottom on the right side and push the needle down through the top left corner to make a cross and then up through the square's lower right corner.

A large velvet cushion was made even prettier with an appliqué that was created with some fabric from a classic pattern by Josef Frank.

The fringe and seam give the appliqué that little bit extra.

Appliqué with Fringe

We purchased this large floor cushion and decorated it very simply. We fringed the edge of a strip of a nice, slightly more expensive fabric and then sewed it onto the cushion. This is a good solution if you want to treat yourself to a more expensive fabric without having to spend too much.

Measure and cut a strip from the fabric to use for the appliqué.

Fringe the edges by pulling the threads away from the material until the fringe reaches the desired length.

Sew the appliqué onto the cushion using a zigzag stitch.

Rug Decorations

Here are some examples of embroidery and decoration:

Sew straight stitches with a slightly thicker yarn and a thick needle.

Cut bits of material about 1 inch (2 cm) wide and 2 inches (5 cm) long, and thread them through the warp of the rug one by one. Space them out equally to make them look like small ribbons.

Rip bits of fabric about ½ inch (1 cm) wide and sew straight stitches with them.

Use yarn to make cross stitches.

Thread 2–3 bits of yarn about 4 inches (10 cm) long through the rug and tie a knot with the yarn to make a tuft.

Be inspired by our stitches and decorations or create your own.

We took a regular white rag rug that we found in the cupboard and brought out lots of yarn remnants and bits of old fabric. Then, we simply started to embroider and decorate the rug. We used simple stitches, tied on some bits of yarn, attached pieces of fabric to the rug warp, and so on. Every row was improvised—nothing was planned. It took a while to finish the whole rug, but it was fun while it lasted.

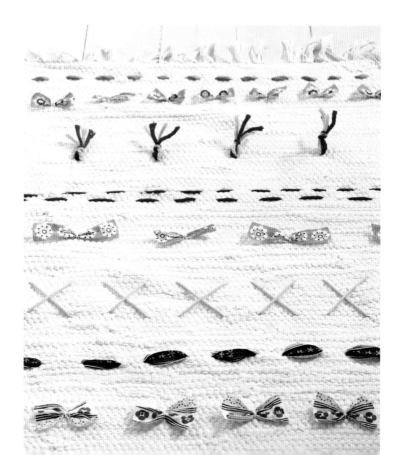

This charming
rug works
well in the
bedroom at
the cottage.

A Trendy Tie

This tie is a vintage find and is probably quite old. It was given our personal touch with embroidery, and then it became the perfect birthday present for a man turning 50. *La vie est belle*—life is beautiful.

Think of what you want to write.

Cross stitch patterns for letters can be found online.

Sketch your embroidery on a piece of paper.

Pin a piece of mesh fabric onto the tie.

Embroider in cross stitch according to the pattern. Page 38 shows you how to make a cross stitch.

Moisten and remove the mesh.

The tie was a much-appreciated gift for a 50th birthday and is frequently worn.

Baker

Most people probably have an apron hanging somewhere in the kitchen. Get it out and add an embroidered pocket. It's an easy starter project for someone new to embroidery. Choose a checkered material to embroider on as it's much easier to get it straight and looking nice.

Measure and cut a piece of material that will be large enough for the pocket, and add a seam allowance all around.

Embroider the words that you have chosen in cross stitch. Use cotton thread in a color you like. Page 38 demonstrates how to cross stitch.

Fold in the seam allowance and press the edges of the pocket. Sew onto the apron.

Now we're baking! Here we have decorated a ready-made apron with a little pocket embroidered with a favorite Swedish phrase . . .

We chose a material with small squares for the pocket. This makes it easier to embroider the letters in a straight and neat fashion.

Measure and cut the material so it fits the bed.

Hem the valance at the bottom and sew a casing along the top edge.

To place the valance around the bed, pull some strong elastic through the casing.

Decorate the valance with a border that can be sewn on using a straight seam.

The border was made from beautiful Indian ribbon, but you can find something similar in most shops. Sew the ribbon on using a straight seam.

A Valance with a Border

Give your bed a makeover with a decorative valance. Most stores don't have a great supply of valances, so it's better to make your own. With a pretty linen fabric in bright pink, this bed now looks delightful.

The new valance looks great paired with a throw with an elephant appliqué. The pattern for the crocheted rug can be found on page 35.

When traveling, keep an eye out for pretty fabric and ribbons.

Isn't it pretty, the whimsical elephant that adorns this cushion? The picture on the wall was sewn as a patchwork quilt from vintage fabrics and was then mounted on a piece of Styrofoam. You can find out how to make the patchwork quilt on page 64.

Feel free to blend patterns and colors for a great mix.

The Cutest Elephant

This green pillow was decorated with appliqué in the shape of an elephant. You can either sew your own pillow case or use a single-colored one you already have. Our elephant shape was cut from an old '70s-era sheet that we bought at a thrift store. The icing on the cake was the crocheted ear and tail.

~~~~~~

Cut out the shape of an elephant in a contrasting material.

Using a zigzag seam, sew the elephant onto the pillow case.

Crochet an ear:

Crochet 5 chain stitches and make a closed ring with a slip stitch in the first chain stitch.

Round 1: Crochet 8 single crochets by going into the ring.

Round 2: Make 2 single crochets in every single crochet.

Rounds 3–5: Increase by 8 stitches distributed evenly on each round.

Rounds 6–7: Continue crocheting 2 rounds without increasing.

Finish off with a slip stitch, cut the yarn, pull through, and secure.

Tail:

Crochet the desired number of chain stitches. Cut the yarn and pull through.

Sew the ear, tail, and a button for an eye onto the pillow case.

We used Soft Cotton yarn and a 4/E hook.

The fabric used for the lettering comes from an old thrift store sheet. Sew the lettering on using zigzag stitches. It doesn't matter if the edges fray slightly—it just adds to the charm.

A pretty pillow with an uplifting message. The bed spread was bought in India.

Decide what you want to write.

Use a computer and printer to print out large letters. These are roughly 6 inches (15 cm) in height.

Cut out the letters to make a template.

Put them on the reverse side of the material and trace them. Remember to place them "mirror imaged."

Cut out the letters.

Pin them onto the cushion cover.

Sew them on using a zigzag seam.

Appliqué is fun and allows for a lot of variety. Just making letters and words is quite popular, and you can get help from a computer and printer when making templates. Give cushions a personal touch by using names or uplifting phrases. Buy premade cushion covers or sew them yourself. You can also use regular pillow cases.

Ravishing Ribbons

Collecting pretty ribbons is fun and they can be used for many different things. When traveling to countries like India and Thailand, you can pick and choose and buy many different ones. But even in your home country there are many great options, even if they are a bit more expensive. This monochrome skirt got revitalized when it was decorated with lots of ribbons. We counted 16!

Plan which ribbons to sew onto the skirt, and hold them against the skirt to see how it looks.

Measure and cut the ribbons.

Pin them onto the skirt.

Sew on the ribbon using a sewing machine.

With a few ribbons, a monochrome skirt was transformed into a folksy skirt.

Sewing & Creating

In this chapter, we look at the fun and useful things we have sewn and created for the home. The ideas are simple, and you don't need to be a professional seamstress to make them.

As usual, we have mainly used fabrics that we already had at home or that we bought at thrift stores. Among other things, fabric remnants, old tablecloths, and secondhand sheets have been transformed into cushions, curtains, and cuddly toys.

We left a pile of fabric topped with pretty ribbons out on a chest of drawers. Why? Because it looks good!

Measure the windows so you know what size your curtains need to be.

Place the tablecloths out on the floor to see what they will look like.

Smooth the tablecloths by ironing them.

Pin them together.

Sew them together with a sewing machine and adjust the tablecloths so that they fit the window and windowsill's measurements.

Sew a casing along the top edge.

Place the curtain on a curtain rod.

A Tablecloth Curtain

In our opinion, old beautifully embroidered tablecloths are works of art that should be taken care of. You can find lots of them at thrift stores. One way to get good use out of them is to make something new—a curtain, for example, can be very attractive!

First, cut the large piece of fabric that is going to be the frame. Ours is about 30 x 50 inches (80 x 130 cm).

Hem the edges.

Cut out the desired number of pockets in different sizes. It's better if you mix the materials as well as the sizes of the pockets.

To make the pockets more stable, place the material for one pocket with the right sides together and sew three of the edges.

Turn the pocket the right way around and hem the last edge. Pin the pocket onto the frame.

Do the same with all the pockets and then sew them on.

Decorative wall storage made from textiles.

Wall Storage

Sew storage pockets to hang on the wall for putting away small items. It's both cute and practical and it works just as well in the hall as in the office or nursery. For the pockets you can use cheap fabric remnants or find bargains at the thrift store.

Hippo

You can make a lot of different things from old sheets (as this book makes clear!). Why not sew a cute hippo with crocheted ears and a tail . . .

Fold the fabric and cut out an animal shape.

Place the pieces right sides together and sew together, leaving a small opening.

Turn inside out and fill with stuffing to pad out. Sew the opening closed.

Embroider the eyes using a couple of stitches.

Crochet two ears

Make 5 chain stitches and make a closed ring with a slip stitch in the first chain stitch.

Round 1: Make 8 single crochets by going into the ring.

Round 2: Make 2 single crochets in every single crochet.

Round 3: Increase by 8 single crochets, evenly distributed.

Round 4: Crochet the round without increasing.

Finish off by using a slip stitch, cut the yarn, pull through, and sew on the ear.

Tail

Crochet the desired number of chain stitches, cut the yarn, and pull through. Sew on the tail.

The Window Seat Cushion

The best and most attractive cushion for your window seat or bench can easily be made at home. This will allow you to choose both size and design. Be inspired by the cushion that adorns our window seat—it gives us a really cozy corner!

Measure and cut the pieces of fabric to your desired size: one top piece and one bottom piece as well as a strip for the edge. This cushion measures 50 inches (130 cm) in length, 16 inches (40 cm) in width, and 2.5 inches (6 cm) in height. Add about ½ inch (1.5 cm) seam allowance around all sides.

Place the parts right sides together and sew together, leaving one of the short sides open.

Turn the right way around.

Stuff the cushion with filling. One cost-effective way is to use the filling from IKEA's cheap pillows.

Finally, sew together the last side from the right side.

To give the cushion a lovely finish we made a decorative seam and created 12 pompoms from yarn, which were sewn on using tight stitches. See page 56 for instructions.

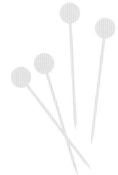

This long cushion is a lovely addition for a window seat, and it's very comfy to sit on.

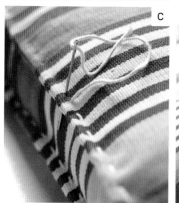

A. A hand stitched edge and pompoms give the cushion some extra flair.

B. The edge with the decorative seam makes the cushion look finished and professional.

C. This simple decorative seam was made using Soft Cotton yarn and straight stitches.

D. Wind the yarn over three fingers—the more yarn you wind around, the denser the ball will be. Pull your fingers out and tie the bundle together. Cut both ends.

E. Sew the pompom straight through the cushion to pull it together. Using a needle, thread the tail end of the yarn through the cushion and tie on the underside to secure.

Sitting pretty!

A pillow with a button decorated in velvet gets a luxurious and finished feel.

Make a cushion cover or use a ready-made one.

Insert an inner pillow into the case.

Dress a button with the material you have chosen according to the instructions on the packaging.

Using a needle and thread, thread the button through the whole cushion, pull tight, and attach to the underside of the cushion.

Cushion with a Decorative Button

We made a luxurious velvet cushion with a decorative button. It looks great on the bed when paired with the stripy cushion. To dress buttons is fun, and you can mix and match them according to your liking. Plastic buttons that can be covered can be purchased from most haberdashers.

Plastic buttons that can be covered with material can be found at the haberdasher's.

57

Measure and draw a triangle on a piece of cardboard or thick paper in the size you want the flags to be. (These are 8 x 9½ x 9 ½ inches [20x24x24 cm]).

Cut out the cardboard triangle to make your template.

Place the template on a piece of folded fabric and trace.

Cut out the desired number of flags.

Place the flags wrong sides together and sew together from the right side up.

Cut a long, thin piece of material and fold it double.

Pin every flag inside the folded strip of cloth and sew them all secure with a straight seam from the right side of the material. Let the edges fray—it just adds to the look.

Some pretty bunting looks great outside the greenhouse.

Fancy Bunting

We are setting the table outside the greenhouse for a party in the sun, and this is the perfect place to hang bunting made from old bits of fabric, thrift store finds, and old clothes. Bunting looks great both inside and out—even when there's no party going on!

This bunting
is made
from fabric
remnants,
sheets, and
old clothes.

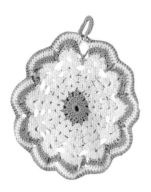

Cushions from Sheets & Pictures from Pot Holders

We really like old, colorful '70s style patterns and it seems as if it's impossible to get bored of them. At thrift stores you can find old sheets with these patterns, which is like finding a treasure. Here is our cache from going the round of thrift stores. We discovered both sheets and crocheted pot holders.

Look through thrift stores for attractive materials.

Cushion

Measure the cushion that's to go inside the cover, add a seam allowance, and cut the material.

Sew the cushion cover right sides together. These are sewn in the same shape as a basic pillow case.

Turn the right way around and cover the cushion.

Picture

Cover a frame with some pretty paper.

Frames can be purchased in arts and crafts stores.

Cut the paper and fold around the frame. Attach it to the back using a staple gun.

Use glue or double-sided tape to fix a crocheted pot holder to the center of the picture.

This pea green blanket was bought at a thrift store along with old sheets that were made into cushions. Under this lovely cascade of color there is an old and worn brown cord sofa.

For the Pins

Surrounding yourself with tools of the trade and pretty materials can boost inspiration and creativity. Of course, to sew you'll need a pretty pin cushion and preferably pretty pins too . . .

The prettiest pin cushion is the one you make yourself.

Cut two rounds of a pretty cotton material.

Sew together with the right sides facing each other and leave a small opening.

Turn the pin cushion the right way around.

Stuff with some filling and sew the opening together (use cheap filling).

Using a needle and thread, stitch around the pin cushion and "pull" together a few times. Secure with a button in the middle.

Use old bits of fabric to sew new things.

Cut the material into your required sizes.

Add a seam allowance.

Make sure the pieces are of equal size.

Make a zigzag seam around all the pieces.

Lay the pieces out to see how they'll look and make sure they add up to a total measurement of about 60 x 80 inches (150 x 200 cm): the size of an average blanket.

Sew the patches right sides together to make a complete piece.

Sew the whole square onto a blanket. We got a cheap one at IKEA.

Sew a button onto each corner—it makes the material stay in place and it also looks cute.

A Patchwork Quilt from Sheets

At secondhand shops, auctions, and thrift stores, you can find old sheets at a good price—sometimes whole boxes filled with these treasures. This patchwork quilt is made from old sheets from the '70s.

A wonderful patchwork quilt sewn from colorful sheets. The patchwork is sewn onto a white IKEA blanket.

Sew buttons onto the corners. This keeps the material in place and also looks good. Feel free to mix and match the buttons.

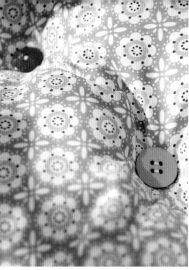

A pretty cushion for
your garden furniture is
easy to make yourself.

Summer Cushion

Cozy cushions for your garden furniture are fun to make yourself, and you're totally free to choose both size and material. We usually use cheap filling. Add a few pretty buttons and the cushion is ready for use.

Measure how big you want the cushion to be and add a seam allowance of ½ inch (1.5 cm). Cut out the fabric. Fold the fabric double to make a square. Ours measures 16 x 16 inches (40 x 40 cm).

Place the material right sides together and sew together the edges, leaving a small opening.

Turn the cushion the right way around and stuff with filling.

Sew the opening together from the right side.

Add five buttons to the cushion. Sew them through the cushion, then pull tight and secure on the underside to pull the cushion together.

Magazine Rack

The back piece

Fold the material double to make it sturdier.

Measure and cut the fabric according to your size requirement.

Sew together three sides, right sides toward each other, and then turn the piece the right way around.

Sew the opening shut.

Fold the fabric and sew a casing at the top edge to fit a thin wooden rod.

The pockets

The pockets can be made from pieces of fabric or you can do what we did and rescue a prettily embroidered tablecloth from a thrift store.

Pin the cloth onto the back piece.

Sew the pockets onto the back piece with four evenly spaced seams and let the fabric/cloth "crinkle" to create sections where you can place the magazines.

Hang the magazine rack on the wall using two hooks that you screw onto the wooden rod.

Make a practical and decorative magazine rack to hang on the wall. We used an embroidered tablecloth that had the right shape and size. We found it at the thrift store. It doesn't get much easier than this.

From a bit of fabric and a secondhand tablecloth we made a lovely magazine rack.

Interior Ideas

We love interiors and creating beautiful surroundings. We love do-it-yourself tips, so we've squeezed in a chapter with a mixture of do-it-yourself projects. We have applied wallpaper, built a bedstead, dressed some boxes, renovated a chair, and more. So be inspired!

Cut the fabric so that it fits both the box and the lid.

Glue the fabric on using craft glue.

Dressed Boxes

You can never have enough pretty storage space. By dressing ordinary paper boxes with colorful fabric, you can create a lovely place to hide away your bits and pieces. IKEA has good paper boxes with lids, but normal shoe boxes work just as well.

Wall Collections

Every crocheted pot holder is a little work of art in itself. It's a wonderful handicraft that mustn't go to waste, and you can often find them for cheap at thrift stores.

We've mentioned our collection of pot holders before, but thought it would be fun to show off these works of art here. One idea of what to do with them is to make a fantastic pot holder wall. It doesn't get better than this!

These pot holders look best against a white wall. They can be nailed to the wall with small white nails.

Personal and pretty
art made from
tablecloths.

Cloth Pictures

Make your own works of art from textiles with the help of some canvas or wooden frames, beautiful materials, and embroidered tablecloths. This is a great example of how to find a completely new use for the tablecloths. These days we don't use tablecloths in the same way as before, but they're so beautiful. These handicrafts should be shown off.

Cut the fabric or the tablecloths to the desired size.

Staple them onto the back of the frame with a staple gun.

If you're covering a frame with both material and a tablecloth, sew the tablecloth onto the material first before stapling it onto the frame.

Roman Blinds

Roman blinds are a good alternative to traditional curtains or a valance. You can pull them up or down depending on your needs, and they look a bit nicer than a normal roller blind. Our version is very easy to make.

A. For the Roman blind you need fabric, a round pole, and a thin wooden strip (all available at a hardware store), cord, cord toggles, buttons, right angled screws, eyebolts, measuring tape, and scissors.

B. Measure the window and cut the material according to the measurements, adding 4 inches (10 cm) at the top and 4 inches (10 cm) at the bottom, as well as a 1 ½ inch (4 cm) seam allowance. Hem the edges of the material by folding the sides in and pressing them before you sew. Sew a casing at the top edge and one at the bottom edge, adapting the size of the casing to the size of the round pole and wooden strip.

C. Using a saw, cut the wooden strip and the round pole to the same measurements as the curtain's width. Place the round pole through the casing at the bottom and the strip of wood in the casing at the top.

D. Place four eyebolts through the material in the strip at the top; one in the middle and one on each side about 8 inches (20 cm) in. The fourth eyebolt is placed about 2 inches (5 cm) in on the right side.

E. Tie the cord to one end through the right eyebolt placed 8 inches (20 cm) in on the wood. Pull the cord along the back of the curtain all the way down and then up along the front to the eyebolt again. Pull the cord through the same eyebolt. Get some new cord and do the same on the left side. Then take the cord and pull it through the central eyebolt and then to the right eyebolt.

F. Pull both the cords through the eyebolt furthest to the right and add a toggle. Tie together the cords and cut them so you have about 12 inches (30 cm) to spare.

G. Screw two further eyebolts into the strip through the material, about 4 inches (10 cm) in on each side. Screw two right angled screws into the wall. Measure so that the distance is equal to that of the two eyebolts and hang the curtain up on the right angled screws. Finally, screw a button into the wall where the cord can be wound round the window's lower ledge.

H. When you pull the cord, the curtain should be pulled up.

I. The fabric will roll around the round pole.

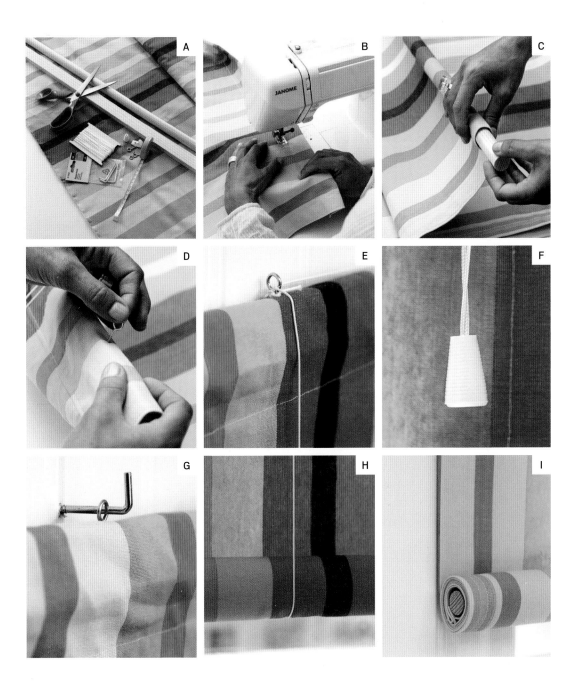

Our Roman blinds are in place and now we can just pull it up or down depending on what we prefer.

After. This chair has been given a new lease on life and we're happy with the result. The description of the crocheted rug can be found on page 35.

Before. A decent chair that was too good to throw away . . .

A Cute Chair

We like to refurbish things. Transforming boring items into something attractive is lots of fun. As an added bonus, you're saving the environment as well as money by reusing old items rather than buying new things. This chair was transformed with some paint and yarn, which makes it look fantastic!

Carefully wash the chair with some TSP (paint cleaner).

Allow to dry.

Lightly sand down with some fine sandpaper.

Paint a base coat, then paint the top coat twice using a paint suitable for furniture.

Crochet a granny square according to the description on page 10 in a size that fits the seat of the chair.

This square was made by doing two rounds in each color for roughly 30 rounds.

The square should be big enough that you can fold it round the edges of the seat.

Staple the granny square to the underside of the seat using a staple gun.

A Beautiful Bedstead

Materials needed

A piece of particle board

Foam rubber

Fabric

Plastic buttons that can be
decorated (can be found
among the sewing items
in craft stores or at the
haberdasher's)

Saw

Screwdriver/screw extractor

Staple gun

Needle and thread

A bedstead makes your room cozy and it makes your bed feel more
enclosed and comfy. Adding a headboard is enough. Try making one
yourself and get inspiration from our bright yellow bedstead in velvet
with decorated buttons.

~~~~~~~~~~~~~~~~~~~~~~~~~~

Use the saw to cut the particle
board to the correct measurement.
Ours is about 50 inches (120 cm) in
height. Sometimes you can get the
board pre-cut at the hardware store.

Cut the foam rubber so that it fits
the size of the board. It should
match the edges of the board. We
used a thin foam rubber mattress.

Cut the fabric and add about 4
inches (10 cm) so that it can be
folded around the particle board.

Dress the buttons according to the
instructions on the packaging.

Place the buttons where you
want them on the fabric and
sew them through both the
material and the foam rubber.
Pull tight and secure on the
back of the foam rubber.

Place the foam and fabric on the
particle board making sure it is
taut, and staple it to the back of
the board with the staple gun.

Using screws, attach the
bedstead to the bed or simply
stand it on the floor behind the
bed.

Didn't we make a lovely bedstead that gives the whole bedroom a boost? The quilt is a secondhand bargain, but you can make your own following the description on pages 10 and 12.

A

B

C

D

A. Plastic buttons are dressed with velvet in bright colors.

B. Sew the buttons through both the fabric and foam rubber.

C. The fabric is secured onto the back of the particle board using a staple gun. The fabric should be pulled taut.

D. Decorated buttons give the bedstead that extra flair.

Take a photo.

Order some wallpaper of the
photo on the Internet. There
are several companies you can
turn to.

Get wallpapering.

A Personal Wall

This is a fun way to create a personal wall that's beautiful to
look at. Take a picture of something you like and make it into
wallpaper. Naturally we chose to photograph a crocheted
blanket. Photo wallpaper can be ordered online and many
companies offer this service. It's easy to use, as all the rolls
are marked, showing how they are to be hung up.

A Happy & Merry Christmas

Christmas is a time for making things. It's just not the same if you don't! You can get far simply by using textiles, but everything from pretty ribbons to crocheted tablecloths and fabric by the yard can be utilized. We like to make new things out of old, and this is true even at Christmas. Rag rugs, lace, and towels can also be used. Remnants in red and white can be made into a patchwork pillow. A basket filled with yarn makes a Christmas decoration. Here we present some quick tips as well as some more advanced ones. Something to remember, though, is to start your crafting early on, as it's much more fun if you don't have to stress over it. You can take your time to make some great Christmas presents.

Christmas spirit is all around. The tree is in place, the table is set, and outside lies a blanket of snow. Merry Christmas!

Yarn as Decoration

Leave your handiwork out and enjoy it as an ornament—even when it's not being used. Our favorite is beautiful balls of yarn in a basket, as it creates a cozy ambiance when you leave it out. It's one of our great tips for decorating. New and personalized labels make them even more attractive.

~~~~~~~~~~~~~~~~~~~~

Remove the original paper labels from the balls of yarn.

Cut some pretty ribbons and tie them around some of the skeins.

Cut some labels out of material with zigzag scissors and attach to the remaining balls of yarn.

Red and white balls of yarn with new labels make for a lovely decorative item.

Pretty Christmas tree decorations made from materials that you can easily sew yourself.

A heart for the tree

Use a gingerbread cutter as a template and trace the shape on fabric that has been folded double.

Cut out the shape, preferably using zigzag scissors.

Sew the pieces together, right way around, leaving a small opening.

Stuff the heart with filling and close the opening together with a ribbon to hang it up with.

Create Christmas spirit with yarn and fabric.

The Heart of the Tree

Creating your own tree decorations is a lovely Christmas activity, and these can be used again and again. A few fabric remnants and some filling is all that's needed. The filling has been taken from a cheap IKEA pillow, which is much more affordable than the filling sold at the craft store.

Christmas Valance

We love pompom fringes and they can be found in great abundance at stores such as Michaels, or among the sewing accessories at a department store. The fringes make a pretty addition to all sorts of things. Here the valance was given a red fringe. The valance was a thrift store purchase that we made a bit more cheery.

Wash and iron the valance.

Measure and cut the fringe so that it matches the measurement of the valance.

Pin the fringe along the bottom edge.

Sew the fringe on using a sewing machine.

> Christmas morning with a porridge breakfast, sitting by the kitchen window under our lovely valance.

Lace & Crochet

Nostalgia at Christmas always works. Crocheted tablecloths are works of art that we think should be treasured. In thrift stores and secondhand shops there are hoards to buy for a great price. What do you do with them? Well there are several options. . . . Sew them onto pillows, bags, bedspreads, or sew them together into an even larger tablecloth. You can also simply lay them out on the Christmas table.

Tie a cute lace ribbon around a vase and place your favorite flowers inside. Set it on a crocheted tablecloth to make your own pretty Christmas arrangement. Here we used some lovely lace from a traditional costume.

Sew together a few crocheted tablecloths using overcast stitching to make a bigger tablecloth.

A lovely sack for Father Christmas to place his presents in.

Thrift Store Bargains

After scouring the thrift stores we came home with a rag rug, a night shirt, and a crocheted tablecloth in red and white. Our discoveries kickstarted our creativity, and these charming items were the result. The night shirt was given new buttons, and with a red ribbon, it made a wonderful Lucia dress to adorn our wall. The rug was made into a floor cushion and the tablecloth was used to decorate Santa's sack.

Santa's sack

Cut a piece of jute into the desired size.

Fold the jute in two.

Sew the edges together using cross stitch with a red yarn.

Decorate using a tablecloth from a thrift store.

Tie the sack together with a ribbon.

Lucia dress

Remove the existing buttons.

Wash and iron the night dress.

Sew on new decorative buttons.

Add a wide, red ribbon.

Hang the Lucia dress on the wall.

The night shirt that we bought at the thrift store was given new buttons and was hung on the wall as a Christmas decoration.

All our thrift store bargains were put to good use.

Sew the rug together using red cross stitching to give the cushion some pretty detailing.

Floor cushion

Fold the rug.

Using a red cotton yarn, sew two sides together using cross stitch.

Place a pillow inside the cover and sew together the opening in the same fashion.

Cushions

New cushions quickly and effectively create a Christmas feel. Search your cupboards at home and use things you already have. Here we have made a patchwork pillow in red and white using fabric remnants. The other ones were made from some tea towels and pretty ribbon.

Patchwork pillow

Utilize fabric remnants.

Cut medium sized squares from a mixture of fabrics but make sure they are the same size.

Pin them right sides together.

Sew them together to make one piece.

Then sew the piece into a cushion cover, a basic pillow case style is the simplest to make.

Place an inner cushion inside the cover.

Isn't it pretty, our patchwork pillow?

With red and white cushions, the sofa is made to feel Christmassy.

Cushion covers made from kitchen towels.

Sew the required number of pretty ribbons onto two kitchen towels.

Sew the two towels together, right sides facing each other, to make a cushion cover/ pillow case.

Turn the right way around.

Place an inner pillow inside the cover.

Sew the last side together from the right side.

Cute Covers

It's fun to set the table elegantly for Christmas and to spend some time getting the decorations just right for the table. Here are some suggestions on how to sew flowerpot covers from kitchen towels. For best results, use good-quality old kitchen towels made of linen.

Fold the kitchen towel in two, lengthwise.

Sew together to make a "tube" to fit your pot.

Cut a piece of contrasting fabric to fit the base and sew it on.

Rosemary is a perfect table decoration at Christmas. We've put some in a pot made from a kitchen towel.

The Christmas hubbub is evident in the kitchen, and the kitchen towels from IKEA with added ribbon are just adorable.

The ribbon is sewn onto the towel using a sewing machine.

Decorate with Ribbons

A packet of two reasonably priced kitchen towels were bought at IKEA and made festive and unique with a pretty ribbon. They're just as lovely to wipe your hands on and dry the dishes with as they are to use as napkins.

Iron the kitchen towels to make them smooth.

Measure the ribbon and cut it according to the measurements of the towel.

Sew the ribbon onto the towel.

In the Jar

This is a Christmas craft that makes a perfect gift. Simply take a glass jar and fill it with something tasty. It can be anything from homemade, healthy muesli to homemade or store-bought candy.

~~~~~~~~~~~~~~~~~

Cut a piece of fabric so that it fits the jar, preferably using zigzag scissors.

Fill the jar.

Tie the fabric on with ribbon, or as we have here, with a pompom fringe.

A charming jar makes a perfect present!

Sleep Well at Christmas

It's nice to make your home look Christmassy, even in the bedroom. During Christmas, we hope you get some time off and treat yourself to a lie in. We decorated this bedroom in red, white, and pink. An old, worn chair adds to the charm and the red and white fabrics on the bed create a Christmassy feel. The bed covers were given that little extra flair by sewing on some lace.

Iron the duvet cover flat.

Measure and cut a piece of lace.

Pin the lace along the edge at the top of the duvet cover.

Sew on the lace using a sewing machine.

A pretty checked duvet set was made even prettier by adding some lace.

Lace & Candles

Tie some lace around a few candles and leave them out as a decoration. Making your home look Christmassy is as simple as that! This batch makes a sweet and useful present as well.

Words are superfluous. We'll let the picture speak for itself.

The Little Lamp

A traditional table lamp was made extra special with a few simple steps. We simply tied an elastic band around the shade, and voila! Changing the ribbon according to the season doesn't have to cost a lot!

Measure and cut the ribbon so it fits around the shade. Glue, tie, or sew the ribbon onto the shade.

We made it Christmassy with a red and white frill.

Sew Your Own Christmas Cards

Using a thicker paper, cut out the size you require—preferably with zigzag scissors.

Fold in half.

Add a decorative seam using a sewing machine.

Sending Christmas cards you designed yourself is a nice gesture for your nearest and dearest, and it doesn't take much longer than going out and buying them. Today's modern sewing machines usually have a host of different decorative seams to choose from, so here we have made some Christmas cards.

Beautiful cards that the recipient will love.

The Different Stitches We've Used:

Chain stitch is abbreviated ch

Make a loop of the yarn. Place the crochet hook into the loop, pull the yarn though to make a stitch, and keep it on the hook. Repeat to get the required number of chain stitches.

Single crochet is abbreviated sc

Start with 1 stitch (st) on the crochet hook. Place the hook into an st and pull the yarn through = 2 st on the hook. Pull the yarn through both st.

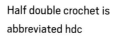

Half double crochet is abbreviated hdc

Start with 1 st on the crochet hook. Place the yarn over the hook, place the hook into an st and pull the yarn through = 3 st on the hook. Pull the yarn through these 3 st at the same time.

Slip, slip, knit is abbreviated ssk

Start with 1 st on the crochet hook, place the hook through 2 st from the previous round = 3 st on the hook, pull the hook through these 3 st all at once.

Slip stitch is abbreviated sl st

Start with 1 st on the hook. Place the hook in a st, pull the yarn through and straight through the st on the hook.

Increasing

Crochet 2 st in the same st.

Double crochet part 1

Start with 1 st on the crochet hook. Place the yarn over the hook, place the hook in a st and pull the yarn through = 3 st on the hook.

Double crochet part 2

Pull the yarn through the first 2 st = 2 st left then pull the yarn through these 2 st.

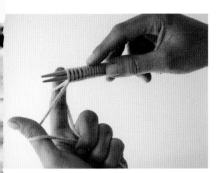

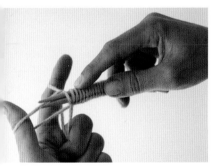

Casting on

The working yarn comes up from the front and is placed around the index finger and between the index and middle finger. The tail of the yarn comes from behind and around the thumb. Hold both bits of yarn against the palm of your hand with the remaining fingers.

The needle is placed through the loop on the thumb from behind and round the yarn from the index finger. Pull the yarn through the loop on the thumb to create a stitch, drop the loop on the thumb, and pull tight. Repeat.

Making a knit stitch

Hold the needle with the cast on stitches in your left hand and place the yarn around your left index finger. Place the right needle into the first stitch coming up from behind and from right to left around the working yarn. Pull the yarn through the stitch on the needle and let go of the stitch from the left needle. Repeat.

Making a purl stitch

Hold the needle with the cast on stitches in your left hand. Hold the yarn in front of the needle around the left index finger. Place the right needle into the first stitch from the front and behind the yarn. Then move the needle from the right to the left of the yarn and pull it through the stitch from behind. Let go of the stitch from the left needle. Repeat.

Binding off

Knit 2 stitches, insert the left needle from left to right into the first stitch made and pull this stitch over the other = 1 stitch left on the needle. Make a new stitch. Repeat.